Tales Of A Dignified Hoodrat

Foreword

I am the voice of disadvantaged youth and it is my duty to express the struggle, love, hate and progression of the young community as a whole by diving into the mental battles, social pressures and constraints that I have experienced in the past and/or currently observe. Some of the constraints
are self-managed, but nevertheless they inflict
the same damage.

Advancement is the goal; stagnation is the enemy.

Pedestal

Breathtaking, mesmerizing, immeasurable.
Black brethren are put down while others are
put
   on
     a
     Pedestal...

---Centuries without shackles,
but the playing field has yet to be leveled.

Where I'm from

The disgusting,dangerous, distinctive masterpiece
of the state.
I arrive home to get some sleep;
 to gunshots I shall awake.
The heartache of losing a relative to a hot piece of
lead is a feeling so many people here have endured.

Daily you're forced to play dodge-bullet with the
neighbors.
My cousin lost, catching one to the head.
Durham is retrogression in disguise, tore down and
renovated in order to be gentrified.
It still swallows the ignorant and spits out the wise,
leaving both for dead.

I guess I'm enlightened, while my perspective of
right and wrong has widened.
What's bad to you may not be bad to me,
cause' I'm used to seeing lost souls stay lost;
never living up to what they could be.

I have felt terror

The gunshots that rang and left
everyone in inquisition, left me
trembling.
I was not used to living on the bottom,
but the shots acquainted me quickly.

I was nine at the time the bangs took my security
and left me defenseless.
The rings were so loud that I questioned if the
bullets would find me eventually.
Momma tried to comfort me, but
there was no use since the bullets sounded too close
for comfort
and the whole situation was
detrimental to my comfortability.
Those 20 shots introduced me to warfare and
successfully tainted me.

A wicked welcoming to hell.

Reporting from the bottom

A warrior I am
Weak I am not,
for battles have plagued
my entire existence.

Never visibly vulnerable,
knowing there aren't many escapes from this
hell I call home.
Along with the prospect of dying poor,
my mental stability is nonexistent.

Brotherhood is a rarity,
for the bottom has turned
everyone's hopes to shit.
Few make it to higher standing,
thinking the bottom is it;
relying on government assistance.

The hunger filled days and restless nights
are never to be forgotten.
I dream of higher ground,
as I report from the bottom.

Recurring Heartache

It is not the bullets that terrify me.
It is the harsh reality my son will
become accustomed to, that causes
the chills to visit.
I envision dying at the hands of the law, and
with every new instance this shameful misfortune
becomes more vivid.
With every new instance my skin feels less like
a source of pride, and more like a form of
imprisonment.
Still oppressed, rarely reaping a benefit
from this system designed to limit
my progression.
At this very moment I am left
defenseless, as my skin
still remains viewed a weapon.

Sore but never soaring

Birds can't soar with clipped wings.
Out of the mud, from the bottom.
They see no other options,
so they scheme.

He without sin may cast the first stone, while
boys on the bottom may cast bullets just for the hell
of it.
In hopes of staying afloat
wicked deeds are what they pursue.
Others see this, but don't see the houses that lack
soap and baby boys going without shoes.

A crucial experience to endure,so
the seeds of a positive future are never
planted into the mind.
Coming from the bottom, food is put above a study
session, a key reason why being upright is
sometimes rejected in order to survive.

Soaring is unattainable with clipped wings
and isn't even contingent when getting
above ground is damn near impossible.

The trenches made savages out of lawyers,
educators and businessmen because of adaptation.
They put the books down and picked up bad habits,
or they burned them for warmth
because the house gets
frigid when there ain't no heat in December.

My boys won't soar with clipped wings, so

their progression is forever hindered.

Life is paradise when you're not
targeted, but
on the other end is travesty.

Dark clouds

Blazed to help cope.
2 years without hope
feels like an eternity, so a
void is present internally.

This life phase is called dark.
Nothing more, nothing less.
I just sparked another one to alleviate
my heart, with my back
against a wall.

I've been on the ropes
watching life kick my ass,
my heart full of spite as I remember the
ghost of joy's past.

I can't fall any lower,
I don't want to be sober.
So I won't be until Dark is over.

Things to live for

Coming to terms with my void as I seek
the things that make my skin tingle.
I have been avoidant of interaction lately,
deterring me from developing connections or
falling out of love with being single.

I love the uncertainty of life and its
shapeless potential as I move
independently through it,
 gaining credentials.
I realize my obsession with cheap thrills.

Centered around a good time because I feel
a sense of belonging when mischief is involved.
A thrill seeker I remain as
my days remain abundant.
I strive to appreciate the lows
even when I have an absence of mind.

Caught in a life of disarray, as tomorrow
has no bearing on today.
I can only hope my days
that remain make me appreciative
of the world's perceived abundance.
Until then a cheap thrill is
what I will chase, and not a day will go to waste.

Headstart(Babycrip's introduction)

A jolly two year old
With a blue bandana finessed onto
his head.
They called it cripping early.
They warped his feeble mind to hold onto
Inhibiting traditions, and his loved ones
would only bare witness.

As the jolly two year old turned
into a trappin twelve year old,
his intentions continued to lose
their purity.
The thought of another route
was never taught to baby crip,
so his mentality remained crippled.

He'd been in the field six
years by the time he turned 18,
So soon he would be big homie.
His early involvement played
to his advantage.

Now bigcrip has kids coming
to him looking to be managed and
damaged.
Inhibiting knowledge he must
Pass, all because he got a head start
in a treacherous life.

If they comin' for me(Baby crip's monologue)

Im covered in the protection of
my glock nine.
If any nigga is after blood,
he won't find mine.
If any boy tries me, it's my glock's
time to shine.
It's that unlucky boy's claim to fame.
This glock can erase a life and
forget a name.
It has forgotten a name or two
because my finger is hard to contain.

I have been tested and tried, but I remain
the same because
a nigga like me is built to last.
They want to take me away from earth, so
I have no choice but to blast.
If these words I convey are my last,
I pray that times like these don't continue.
I can hope for change, but not without
my judge on my hip.
I could take it off and sentence an unlucky soul
to death, plastering his face on shirts that
say r.i.p.

Deadly Depression

He's a corpse
putting on a facade,
faking smiles, dreading tomorrow.
When tomorrow comes, he's never ready
and never optimistic; until in the presence of others.
Not even his mother can get through to him.
She recognizes his battle
because she knows when her son is really at peace.
She sees his body language, and views a face of
defeat.
He can't feel the love his loved ones express to
him.
He tries to push them away instead.
He has angels surrounding him,
but demons live in his head.
This is why he feels dead.

Don't take another step

The jig is up and it's all over.
I tremble and struggle to hold
my composure,as immense adrenaline has
made my soul a deadly boulder

The weight is on my shoulders,
the same ones I'm peeking over.
I know it's over.
Everything feels like a blur, but I can hear the
officer's commands
from where they stand.

They told me to drop the weapon, my last line of
defense.
I contemplate resistance, as I know
I almost got off with my life and the cash.
If I don't shoot my way out of this situation I'll
think about the alternate
ending, never to be forgotten .
It's two cops with fatal shots in their sights.
Lift my arm, I lose my life.

They're advancing toward me, flashing their
blinding flashlights and guns with beams.
My only exit is backward because they failed to
surround the scene.
They won't hesitate to neutralize me, I can hear it
in their voices.
I begin to think about how this all could have been
avoided.

Never will I be in this situation again, so I have to
make my move quickly.

I turned and now i'm running with the boys on my
rear, thinking about
staying clear of the only institution I fear.
They're commanding me to stop, but I refuse.
I start to hear pops behind me and I now realize
that my life is what i'm about to lose.
I thought I would make it to 21, but
the end for me is closer than next year; or even
next-

What privilege

Privilege doesn't come across the
poverty line,
nor does it travel to darker pigments.
The fruits of black labor amount
to more labor for limited progression,
as others soar with less effort.

Privilege don't come in Black, preventing
any dark royalty from wearing it.
I don't care to have it because I won't
be a have-not for too much longer.
In reality, the morality of white privilege
is all wrong; but it's a recurring, and treacherous
song.

Lift Our Spirits

You took control of rowdy America.
We were as blissful as we could be.
Relieved,
for a moment.

We had to face the fact that you couldn't change a
system that wasn't created for minority people
initially.
This caused some of us to look at you more bitterly.

Nevertheless, most of us remained faithful.
You were our safety net. Our protector.
Our diamond. Our beacon of excellence.
When you were inaugurated the second time,
It felt as if we all had become president.

I was a little older then, so
I could appreciate you more.
I was inspired.

Now I'm left wanting, and
wishing you were still our safety net and protector.
But you will always be our diamond
and beacon of excellence.

I'm seventeen now, and I appreciate you most now
that you're gone.
I'm infiltrated with a feeling of bittersweetness
when reminiscent
of the two times you were elected in November.
Regardless of my feelings, it's evident
you will be missed,
and remembered.

Nowhere to go.. but up

Ignorance can't amount to bliss when it comes to
this.
I need an out, because
the streets keep tormenting me and
leaving me sick.

The bird in disarray

No longer feeling the joy of childhood,
as the support you were dependent on
forces you to fly from a nest that never quite
made it onto a branch.

You have to work to appease your hunger
or you'll depend on handouts.
Never wanting to be a social standout or outcast,
secluded by monetary limitations.
These are the thoughts of bird that
must learn to fly from a dysfunctional nest.
A bird on solid ground can't stay around for long
and
I know most birds on the ground pray to die, to be
relieved from the misery of failed flight.

My right wing is bruised and my left leg is scarred.
Still I must fly far
and fly high.

I have been trained

I have been trained
to combat my feelings with
over aggression and things alike.
Hard shell, vulnerable core so I
seldom feel the tendencies I
constantly fight.
I'm unstable and hoping this isn't preventing
me from flight, for my emotions
rarely see the light of day.

All I know is struggle, so I know no other height.
My muddy perspective makes me resent my
plight furthermore.
My perspective remains a daunting sight, as I
understand the pits of life.
They understand me too,
knowing what they created.

Struggle and I have known eachother up until
today,
so my only option is to be resilient day to day.
My resilience is acquainted with a moratorium
of feelings, so pardon my emotional distance.
I'm just making my way.

Lost

In a cloud of apprehension as
thoughts of disorientation
plague my mind and daily life,
forcing me to look toward relief.
I've been searching for tools and
 keys to a better life, but the benefits
have yet to find me.

In this bubble of descension.
Exactly why smoke clouds plague my decisions
and routines, because I need something to lift me
up,
 leave me suspended or stuck with glee.
Not a single day has seen the best version of me.

Not a single person has seen my pinnacle.
As I coast and tread in this sea of normality I see
that a lost soul like mine can't help but to be
abnormal.
A benefit has to reap from the struggles I endure
constantly, which strive to strip me of my self
belief.

I try to remain patient and accepting of life's
perceived abundance, but the stagnation
persists; mercilessly leaving me distraught.

I will relish the day my purpose is fulfilled and my dream is caught.

Aware

When pushed to the edge but led astray,
it's hard to find better ways.
Dancing with danger isn't
so hard to a vessel
who endures hardship daily.
To a man on the brink of starvation
who lacks everything but ability,
the American dream is just stability.

Real is respected since
life has shown him nothing but reality.
Life has shown him
nothing but pain.
His reality is an undying strain,
and his pain controls his
undying thoughts.
His thoughts are doubting his own
progression because his reality has not
shown him better.

His pain stems from more
than physically, lacking but
he is mentally set on sustenance;
for a dream is nothing but a
distraction from duties.
Dreaming costs, and he
doesn't have the financial backing.

He has to get off of the ground before any dreaming can happen.

Reaching

There is nothing authentic around me.
Only things real on earth which I feel,
are God's lessons.

Phony pastors are still preaching
and I'm still reaching
for something, anything actually.
I need progression to relieve myself of internal
aggression
and depression.

I'm reaching for more because
I can't be another plug outside a corner store.
I can't stay impoverished
so I'm reaching;
not for money entirely, because
it is true happiness that I have hopes of acquiring.

My wingspan is tremendous, though
I don't know where to reach.
 Regardless I am.

Something has to give, or I give up.
I have to learn how to live, and not try to
live up to society's standards.

I'm an individual, and I am far more than standard.
I don't want to reach for acceptance of my
individuality
from a world of people who can't
accept their own,
so I'll reach for my destiny from now on.

First step..

The things I was doing were not a reflection of
who I'm striving to be.
Dropping those habits made positivity
come easier to me.

Doin right don't make you righteous

Righteous as of now,
trying to steer right along the straight and narrow.
Curvy women and good drugs embody my
temptation.
Trying to launch from the slums but I can't gather
my footing,
plus the hood doesn't make a good launching pad.
What would help is a better foundation, but
since that's a lost cause I feel lost at times.
I said lost, not defeated.
Visions of mediocrity scare me into action, because
there is nothing gained from being stagnant
except hardship.

My heart aches for my brothers' current condition
but I can not stay here to experience it firsthand.
Elevated thinking to elevated living is the only
thing
for which I stand.

Burned bridges is not a part of the plan
but I know change breeds spite.
I'll accept the burned bridges if they're used
to cross into a better life.

Ambiguous

Need I say more
while giving less of myself
to people who take me for granted.
My soul had to do a few laps
before realizing It needed repair
stat.
It took me long enough to gauge
the amount of damage.

The cat is out of the bag, while
I'm out of my comfort zone
and reality.
Am I growing or coasting?

The cost of progression is much more
than time,
though time is of the highest value.
It has always been too difficult for
me to finesse.
I feel it pushing me along,
alone and it feels meaningless;
such as life, a ball of ambiguity
that I was, and still am too
conflicted to try and figure out.

While I give less to people
and more to ambiguity,
I hope to grow because I need an out.

Close is for horseshoes

If it can be viewed in the mind
 it can be held in hand.
A lot of things should
diminish in value as one
strives to be a better man,
or improve his standing.
Things get hard, but a persistent soul is built to
surpass.
Things get hard, but trials don't last;
whether good or bad.
One must weather any storm, whether
inhibited or enabled.
A persistent mind enables anyone of flesh
to strive for success.
Work becomes the acquaintance of a
soul never at rest.
Different attempts for the same goal as
one scratches and crawls to
reach a higher plateau.
Once reached it doesn't suffice
for long.

To a visionary,
life is but a constant
climb.

Where did spirituality go

Value of a dollar diminishes once
The value of spirituality heightens

Paper isn't worth one's well being,
but being that it's currency…

Currently everyone is going with
the current of the workforce where
companionship does not come into play.

We're all in an avoidant day and age of love,
but spirituality is what I will not continue to
forsake.

Transition to thriving

From fighting to flourishing.
From shootings to stocks..
I will never fold and
my growth will never stop

Here I stand

I didn't mean to drop hints of dissatisfaction,
as I was unaware of the situation's severity.
I meant to be appreciative of your kindness
because a bigot with power is such a rarity.

I didn't mean to prosper,
climb out of poverty or not
know my role as an aide to you.

I didn't recognize, for it's not my role.
I'm a role model to kids and a symbol
of success, in the slums where it seems
nobody can progress.
I concoct more from less in ways too
complex for most to fathom.

An acquired taste for success pushed
me out of the social abyss, into a position
to gain respect.
I just couldn't settle for less.

Letter to Ty..

Once too scared to fly.
You would rather sleep in when
the depression deepened, which
resulted in thoughts too raw to
withstand.
On the brink of leaping,
hearing the devil creeping and
your own demons accompanying
you, a confused young man.
At your darkest point, the world's
evils felt empowered, because
you were buried at first glance.

Now here you stand.
Bruised and imperfect, but
nevertheless a helping hand.
You stand alone it seems, but with a
stronger grasp of things like the
disoriented man.

God made you face all of the
problems from which you initially ran.
Only this time, equipped
with love, it benefitted you to
withstand them.

Made in the USA
Middletown, DE
21 July 2023

35199522R00024